DEFINING MOMENTS

Reclaim Your Power
&
Live The Life You Love

Anna M Stapleton

Contents

Introduction

The flavour and quality of our lives can be summarised in the defining moments that we all experience. Those moments go from one extreme to another, from happy and constructive to heart breaking and devastating. By sharing these moments, we make life richer for ourselves and the people around us.

These defining moments happen at all stages in life. For me, the most recent one was receiving my first pension payment. I realised that I would no longer have to earn money to make a living. I felt thankful for receiving the money, yet, at the same time, I experienced a sense of sadness and resentment. Yes, where has time gone! Within a few minutes my whole life flashed through my mind.

Setting the scene

This book is for those who believe at a deep level that we choose where our life goes. Most people do, yet we all have obstacles — some obvious, some invisible — that prevent us from taking the level of control that we know we need to make the most of our lives.

I see myself as part of the generation of baby boomers who have spent years in a period of economic growth. If you are like me, you may feel you have succeeded but you are still hungry, you want something new and different, something that can give you the power to deal with the new challenges that face you:

ageing, children leaving home, the arrival of grandchildren, retirement and parents dying.

Or maybe you are taking your first steps in a new environment or new phase of your life. You can sense your path ahead but it is foggy and winding. If only you could stop and take the time to build a steady foundation, you might go ahead into the unknown with confidence.

With the knowledge and experience gained through spending many hours within the personal growth, training and development environment and years in the world of work, I have adopted the approach of life coaching where, rather than giving answers, I show you how to find your own. It is your agenda and your responsibility to choose what steps to take and I can guide you through the process.

To find your answers and fulfil your goals, I ask you to make full use of technological advances and the abundance of information now available to all of us. There are no real excuses for not finding ways to overcome the obstacles that you face. As someone once said to me: 'Don't believe anything I say, just be willing to try it on!'

The first step is to start the process of putting yourself into a space where you can choose with clarity and reflect on your life without judgement.

This space is not physical; rather it refers to a clear mental gap between your thoughts and your actions. Developing this space is the key to making choices that are consistent with how you want to be known in the world. The gap needs to be wide enough to provide clarity and allow you to consider your next move, whilst not too long to risk allowing your old conditioning to influence you and fall back into the inertia of old habits.

This is particularly important in your communication with others. Rather than reacting to what has been said, this space is where you can remind yourself of who you want to be in the world, and choose a response that is consistent with that commitment.

Take, for example, how I want to relate to my children. I want to be known as a committed mother who loves them unconditionally. When I communicate with them on a day to day basis, I do all I can to keep myself in an empowering space, continually asking myself: 'Is what I am saying or the way I behave, consistent with what I am committed to as a mother?' Although not necessarily perfect, my relationship with them is a healthy one.

This space that I am referring to is not just for communicating with others, but also with yourself. It is a space where you give yourself time to reflect, to step back and view your life as a whole, looking back at where you have been and ahead to where you are going. Have you been where you want to be? Are you where you want to be now? Are you heading in the right direction? Do you have the wherewithal to put yourself on the desired path? If not, what are the obstacles to fulfilling those goals?

These are the questions I guide you through with my coaching. My intention is not to give you answers; instead, I will help you to discover what matters to you, find the tools to follow your own path and to recognise that it is your job to find the answers.

I like Plato's quote which says: 'You cannot teach a man anything, you can only help him to find it within himself'.

Thank you for taking the time to read this book.

Chapter 1
The Big Fish in a Small Pond

Get Me Out of Here

I always knew the little village I grew up in was too small for me. As a teenager, I would look to the horizon and think to myself, 'I wonder what's beyond those mountains!'

In the early 50s, life was tough in my farming village up in the Apennines to the north-east of Rome. Although we had food and basic necessities, cash was scarce. As a child, I contributed to the running of the farm. It is there that I can find one of my earliest defining moments: the day I lost the cows.

My brother and I were in charge of watching the cows to make sure they did not wander out of our fields and eat our neighbours' crops. At one stage, my brother left me minding the cows. Suddenly, I could no longer see them. They had escaped into the forest, and I followed. I waited for my brother for what seemed to be hours until it was dark. I could not see my brother, let alone the cows.

I was the youngest of the family, and though no one ever said anything to warrant my feelings, I felt I was a burden and had to work hard to justify my existence. Lost and alone in the forest, I became overwhelmed by the weight of the responsibility as I felt unable to control the situation and fulfil the task I had been given.

Eventually, my brother came back and we found the cows, but that heavy feeling of responsibility stuck with me and is still vivid today, over 50 years later. Since then, I have taken all my responsibilities very seriously — I never want to be unprepared and experience that sensation of being overwhelmed ever again.

This defining moment shaped the way I related to responsibility until I discovered that responsibility is not a burden rather, it is a choice, which is something I come back to in a later chapter.

Another defining moment was when I had to buy a notebook for school, something so simple that most of us now would take for granted. But we had no money then, not even for something as simple as a notebook. Instead, my mum gave me two eggs which I could use to trade at the shop.

I walked up to the shop counter, eggs in hand, and the shopkeeper looked down his nose at me and sneered, 'You have no cash, then?'

I looked at the eggs and looked at him and thought to myself, 'You are saying I am poor and I hate you.' After the humiliating exchange, I swore to myself, 'I will never, ever get caught without money, ever again.' To this day, even if I have money in my bank account, I always carry cash in my purse. This attitude drives my husband mad — to him money is money, wherever it is — but I am comforted by the feel of notes between my fingers and the weight of coins in my purse!

I have to admit that many years later when I was told the shop keeper had died, the first thought that came to my mind was, 'At least now he won't be able to tell anyone that I have no money.' That experience was as fresh in my mind then as when I walked out of the shop.

This defining moment has shaped my relationship to money and finance. I can look back in my life and I am proud to say that I have always had enough to pay for what I owe. No one can say that I have no money!

The third major defining moment was my move to London. It was the early 70s and I was just a teenager, and following up on a chance conversation with a friend, I seized the opportunity to set up plans to move away from an environment that, at the time, felt very restrictive.

A family in London was looking for an au-pair. It took a few months, but eventually I had an aeroplane ticket and a letter inviting me to come to London. The instructions were cryptic, I was given nothing but a number to call when I reached Gatwick airport. I called (in fact, I had someone call for me because I could not speak English) and they gave further instructions: go to Victoria station, and wait under the clock at platform 13.

So many little threads of coincidence had led me to London, and there I was, waiting at platform 13 in a city that I would fall in love with. I saw it as a clean slate. I had discovered what I was looking for beyond those mountains.

Although I have no regrets and feel blessed and grateful for all I have experienced, I also want to acknowledge that at the time I neglected the implication of being part of a family and the impact of my departure would have on my siblings, my father and especially on my mother. My hunger for freedom and my limiting belief that I was a burden blinded me from considering how my actions would hurt the people who loved me the most.

As I reflect, what stands out most of all is the sacrifice my parents made to ensure my siblings and I had what we needed, a sacrifice that enabled me to chase my dreams and talk to you today. My parents always said, 'We want what is best for you.' In their simplicity, they have taught me humility and unconditional love, and were role models for commitment and duty. They are part of me and I miss them.

Though my restless, rebellious spirit prevented me from accepting and appreciating what I had at the time, I can now look back and join the dots of all the defining moments that have shaped my beliefs and my mission in life.

I have come full circle. We now own the house I was born in and go there for family holidays. Although the mountains look the same, they do not seem so far away. A beautiful defining moment was when I went into the house and said to myself, 'I have come home.' Words cannot explain how this felt.

I made it! What now?

Let's go back to when I was 19 years old, fresh off the plane in London. I had found my freedom — or at least what I called freedom back then. I had left the safe predictability of the family in Italy for London, where I could wake up every day without knowing who I would meet, what I would do or where I would go.

But was I really free? My definition of freedom has evolved over the years. Many of the times when I thought I was free I was actually stuck in my own invented narrative, a story I was writing for myself every day and the character I had to play based on the experiences of my early years.

What I have learnt through the many roles and many challenges of my life is that freedom is found in letting go of expectations of how things should be and overcoming the resistance towards change; it is found in the moment by moment experience of life when you know that there is love in you and in others. When you can trust in that love, you are liberated.

Striving for true personal freedom takes work. Real freedom is discovered, not given. This is achieved through being engaged in questioning what your daily life consists of, not coming from doubt but coming from wonder.

I want you to consider whether your ways of thinking serve you or whether they hold you back. I also want to help you —

wherever you are in life — get one step closer to discovering what really matters to you.

I say 'closer' deliberately. This is a journey with no final destination. Life is a mountain without a top, it is a continuous process. This process for me will go on until the time comes to leave this place we call Earth.

The defining moments which led to me leaving home, settling down in London and all that followed have shaped the way I want to relate to others as well as to myself.

What are the defining moments that have shaped your life? Are there patterns that you are not clear on or not happy with and want to change? If so, read on.

Chapter 2
Where Are You Now?

Take out your GPS

If you are still reading this book, you may have decided that you want some changes in your life. Good! However, these changes may not come easily. By definition, change means leaving behind something familiar while moving towards something different and possibly unknown. There will be powerful urges, some internal, some external, that will get you to resist change, even if you know that it is the right thing to do.

So that you can make changes, you will need to find new resources of guidance and support, or discover sources of clarity and power existing inside of you that you are not yet aware of.

To do that, you must develop yourself. This development can be physical, mental and emotional. I believe that success is determined by the integration of all three. This may seem an impossible task at first and it will require a willingness to take action despite your reservations.

I will cover in a later chapter what I mean by being willing. For the moment let me emphasise that the willingness to act prepares you mentally in breaking down the real and imaginary barriers to your success. At the same time, you will need a framework within which to operate, which I call context. By clarifying the context of your life together with the willingness to take the actions and with outside support you will reach your goals.

Are you willing? Do you have a context for your life? Are you open to guidance and support? If you are, then let's begin the process, which starts — as with any journey — with figuring out where you are right now.

Make a map of your life

So, where are you? Just imagine yourself standing in the middle of a roundabout. You got there from one of the roads and you now have to choose which exit to take. One will lead towards your goal, others will take you to places you do not want to go, and one will take you back to where you started. In the same way that you look at a map to establish where you are in the country, you need to map out where you are in your life so you can figure out the direction of each of those roads.

In the distance, shining on the horizon is your ultimate goal, your purpose, your reason for being. You might not know what this is yet, but you at least need a rough direction to head in.

Once you have figured out where you are and decided which direction to go, you can establish measurable parameters with starting and finishing points — think of them as milestones on your road to your goal. These will allow you to measure your progress, both making your journey feel more satisfying as well as providing you with evidence of your progress or, if things do not go well, you can obtain feedback, establish what did not work and reconsider your direction.

Is your reality really real?

Before you make a start on your journey on the path that you have chosen, it is useful to make sure that you are seeing reality for what it is, otherwise you could be choosing a path based on goals that you do not truly desire or to avoid problems that do not actually exist. There is often a huge difference between dealing with the facts of physical reality versus what goes on in our heads.

Try to compare the reality of your situation with your feelings about the situation and look for any inconsistencies between the two. This can be incredibly difficult, because reactions that are not based on what is happening in reality, feel just as real as those that are. To separate the two, you need to dig beneath your immediate feelings to uncover false perceptions and bad mental habits that have developed over the years. I refer to them as limiting beliefs which are formed from past conditioning and which I will cover in more detail later in the book.

How successful are you in reconciling the mismatch between your physical reality and your disempowering emotional reactions?

There were times as a teenager when I was very unhappy. I had a generous, loving family and yet I felt unhappy and dissatisfied. It was as though I refused to accept something that I longed for but could not accept. It made no sense.

A turning point was when I understood that those discrepancies were caused by limiting beliefs that were born in defining moments — some of which I can identify, others I cannot, though still feeling their effect. Now that I know this, when I experience a discrepancy between how I feel and my surroundings, I want to discover whether my reactions are based on what is happening right now or whether they are the result of being reminded of something that happened in the past.

It is especially important to find this out when feeling overwhelmed and engulfed by the demands of life. It is then that you are most vulnerable and run the risk of losing focus and become emotionally paralysed.

It is when you reach this point (or preferably, long before) that you must recognise that you are stuck in a rut, not doing things because you want to or because they are best for you, but because you are in a state of inertia and changing habits is too difficult.

What would your life be like if you could train yourself and rather than reacting automatically, your actions were based on what is actually happening and who you are committed to being in life? Or, how would you feel if your actions were based on inspiration rather than the conditioning from past events?

How to establish a sense of perspective

To get a glimpse of how this works, let's go back to one of the defining moments I shared in the introduction, when I felt embarrassed for not having the money to buy a notebook. To this day, my emotional response to my finances is that I feel poor, even if, in reality, I have enough money to be secure. This has caused quarrels with my husband because he could not understand why my emotional experience was contrary to our situation and not enjoying what I have for fear of lack.

To reconcile the difference, I created a mental space so I could take control of my reactions: I could acknowledge what was happening in my head, communicate with my husband so that he could understand the root of the contradiction I was experiencing and, at the same time, I could make sure this contradiction did not disempower me.

This example is a demonstration of what I have covered so far: a defining moment led to a limiting belief, which I recognised as such and was willing to deal with it. I could recognise the contradiction, both within myself and in my relationship with my husband, and then took action to manage it. The interesting part is to note that the root of the problem was not with the present situation with my husband, rather it went back to me going into the shop to barter two eggs for an exercise book.

Personal growth and development come from unravelling the impact of tens, maybe hundreds, of these moments, some big, some small. Gradually, by dealing with these challenges, you can make significant changes within yourself and your relationship with others and the world around you.

Stopping by design

Unfortunately, far too often such changes are not made from a position of stability and power. Rather, we often only reflect after an emergency, such as a health problem, losing a loved one or suffering from any number of traumas or relationship breakups.

Or, we look back only when it is too late to avoid the damage of the impact of those defining moments and resulting limiting beliefs, leaving us with a feeling of regret and powerlessness.

Wherever you are, I urge you to stop. This is what I call stopping by design, putting aside your stresses and worries for a moment to reflect on where you are and on how you got there. What distinguishes human beings from other species is that we have the power of language and self awareness — we do not have to be at the mercy of our circumstances — but if we do the same thing day in day out without taking time to stop and think, we are not making use and therefore benefiting from those qualities that we have the privilege to possess.

Again, let me use an example from my life, this time when I made the choice to transform my relationship with my mother in law. She believed I was not the right person for her son and that if she wanted to see him, she had to put up with me. I felt rejected and unfairly treated. Resentment and anger were present in our interactions.

I stopped by design, asked for support from my own coach, took a look at where I wanted to be, a good relationship, versus where I was, a bad relationship. I created the mental space to generate responses that were consistent with my goal of having an enjoyable relationship with her. Within a short period of time, the quality of our relationship dramatically improved and our lives were better for it. I changed the way I related to the whole situation.

The long term impact of this cannot be understated. In her later years, I had the privilege of being involved with her care. At one time she said to me, 'I don't know how you do it, but you seem to know what I need before I do.' Her comment filled me with joy because it conveyed just how close we had become, to the point that our relationship transcended the need for words.

Now, imagine if I had kept reacting automatically all those years back, adding negativity on top of negativity instead of taking action to break the cycle and work towards a better relationship. I would have never experienced what became one of the most special relationships in my life.

Stopping and making space in your thoughts is how you can re-examine the constituent parts of your life and how each part impacts you individually and as a whole. For me, my relationship with my mother in law was just a small part of my life, but resolving it changed my life, and hers too, for the better without mentioning the very positive impact on my husband and the children.

Before moving on, take a moment to stop by design and assess where you are right now, either using the roundabout or any other analogy you find useful to visualise the paths you have taken in your life and those that are now available to you. Detach yourself from your impulsive thoughts and feelings so that you can map out what is truly happening in your life right now, from your relationship with yourself, to your career or any other areas of your life that matter to you.

Chapter 3
How Did You Get There?

Check your GPS again

Think back to the analogy of the roundabout. The middle of the roundabout is where you are in your life currently. In order to move forward, you need a map of where you are now and how you got there so that you can make an informed decision on what exit to take.

As with being on the roundabout faced with which exit to take, in your daily life you need to do the same: make choices. Inevitably, these choices are influenced by past experiences and your hopes for the future.

Consider that there are two distinct aspects of life to take into account to make sense of how you got where you are. The first aspect relates to us as human beings, common to all of us and the second relates to our specific circumstances; of course, these two aspects are inter-twined.

We are all human beings

It is well documented that, at any one time, we are conscious of no more than 5% of what is happening around us with the other 95% happening automatically and over which we have little control. Truth be told, we do not really know what is actually going on. However, stopping here would be pointless and unhelpful.

In its simplest form it could be said that we operate within two domains, the conscious and subconscious.

The first, conscious domain, consists of what we can observe at a physical level as well as what we perceive at mental and emotional levels. The other, subconscious domain consists of what is going on that we are not aware of and that is automatic.

Both domains, but especially what is going on at a subconscious level, are impacted by other factors: the way the brain works at its most basic function, your current circumstances and your past experiences.

Let us consider the functions of the primary part of our brain. The main function of the primary part of the brain is to protect us through a basic, survival mechanism. When we feel threatened, we defend ourselves by attacking other people, or even ourselves, through instinctive fight, flight or freeze responses. It is a useful mechanism much of the time, but unfortunately it cannot distinguish a real threat from an imaginary one.

Moreover, this specific part of the brain can only learn from past events, so even if our current situation has nothing to do with our past, if the brain perceives it as a threat, it will repeat the same patterns used in the past, thus ensuring our survival. This part of the brain automatically guides us to revert back to what is familiar, even if what is familiar consists of unhealthy and unproductive behaviours.

Another aspect of this part of the brain is that it focuses more on negative outcomes than on positive ones. It is well documented that because of how the brain evolved, negative experiences regularly outweigh positive ones because they are more of a threat to our survival.

Most people will make more effort to avoid loss than to benefit from an equivalent gain. In intimate relationships, it typically takes at least five positive interactions to counterbalance every negative one. For people to begin to thrive in life, positive moments usually need to outweigh negative ones by at least a three-to-one ratio.

Being present to what is going on, exploring our past and being aware of how the human brain works, could provide the wherewithal to make sense of how we operate, how others operate and how we can use this knowledge and awareness to make powerful choices rather than knee-jerk reactions.

We have the power to control what comes out of our mouths. We have the ultimate choice on the language we use to describe ourselves, our circumstances and the people and the world around us. We also have a say on how we express it. These two factors, the language we use and how we express ourselves, reflect our reality.

Irritations that hide unresolved issues

In addition to considering the common aspects of how we operate, we can look at the individual aspects, which can be linked to our defining moments and that brought us to where we are. How can you relate to them in a way that is productive and not regressive? How do you learn valuable lessons from them without slipping into coddling nostalgia?

One possible approach is to establish what irritates you, whether it is something about yourself, about other people or certain situations. The irritations trigger you and act as a magnifying glass.

More often than not, these irritations have little to do with the person you are speaking to or the current situation. Rather, they come from decisions made following defining moments from your past, from conflicts in your memories that you replay again and again because they are unresolved and colour how you view life now.

An irritation is like a fishing pole in your hand, being tugged by unseen forces deep beneath the water. You may not know what is under there irritating you, but if you keep reeling in the line then you can eventually pull up the past event that is still impacting you today.

Take the time to list the top ten things that irritate you in your life, no matter how big or small. Now, look through your list and think of each one and ask yourself, 'When have I felt this feeling before?' Keep looking back further and further and you will see that you may be trapped in a pattern of repetitive behaviour. Your reactions have no real connection with what is actually occurring now, but rather are simply habits that you learned early on and never had the courage, objectivity or necessity to break and create fresh ones.

An example of irritation in my life is when someone talks a lot and looks at me in a disapproving and or disparaging way. I lose the thread of the conversation and get confused. It is necessary for me to catch myself, otherwise I run the risk of getting irritated and shutting down.

Another example, it takes me back to a lecture I attended. Without even interacting with the presenter, I discovered I was irritated by him. He had not even spoken and I felt irritated by the way he looked.

As he started, I was so distracted by his features, that I could not hear a word he was saying. He clearly reminded me of a disempowering encounter from the past. Luckily, I acknowledged that my reaction was nothing to do with the presenter. Instead, I shut my eyes, listened to what he had to say and learned about a topic I was very interested in.

I could have missed out, had I not taken responsibility for my reaction and done something about it, on this occasion the simple act of shutting my eyes. Perhaps he thought I was asleep and not interested in what he had to say, which clearly was not the case!

Do you have examples where you dismiss someone just because of the way they look or speak? Are you missing out because of that?

Remember, your brain is trying to protect you by preventing you from experiencing the discomfort you felt previously. However, you need to uncover the source of your irritations to discover who you really are and, eventually, who you can become.

It is important therefore to recognise that your past experiences, your culture, even your genetic tendencies have made you who you are. The objective is not to abandon your past, but to embrace and understand it entirely. Only then can you avoid making automatic responses to what is happening, and instead make your decisions based on what is best for you and the future that you want. It is as though you observe yourself from the outside, without passing judgements or letting your emotions dictate what you think or how you react.

I want to share another defining moment which, looking back has taught me a big lesson.

It was around the time of the birth of my second child. There I was in hospital and, due to complications during the birth, I ended up in the acute care department for several days. I got very irritated and disappointed with myself. It felt as though I had failed in having a problem free childbirth. My expectation was that my stay in hospital would only be for a few hours.

I was at my most vulnerable, most in need of rest and recovery, but would I admit it? Of course not! Instead, I went back to work soon after, I had to keep going and deal with everything. Within a period of six months it got serious enough that I was at the verge of a nervous breakdown. I was lucky enough to wake up and say to myself: 'What are your doing to yourself?' I adjusted the balance between work and family life and took responsibility for my wellbeing.

I can laugh at it now, but I know that the need for being in control and the fear of not being capable were deep within me. I relate to this period of time as wanting to prove I could deal with anything. Perhaps I was reliving the experience of being afraid and overwhelmed like the little girl in the woods.

You will have you own examples. Take a moment and look back at your life and identify defining moments you can use as lessons to learn from. Think of times you acted in an unhealthy or unhelpful way, or did not stand up for yourself, or put effort into something that did not turn out the way you wanted. From the safety of the present, look into the past and try to identify those moments and ask why you acted the way you did. If you do, you will see a pattern emerging. How can you break that pattern?

Going from children to adults

We talk about children and adults as if there is a defining line between the two, but we never lose the child within us. Acting as if we are now adults and draw a line to put our childhoods behind us, is short sighted and ignores how the impact of the experiences of defining moments as children, continues in adulthood.

For example, at some point when I was very young, an adult made a disparaging remark about a birthmark on my forehead. I cannot remember who said it or when, but the tone of that remark stuck with me, and made me feel like a freak.

Another example is when, in my teens, someone inappropriately complimented me for my 'generous breasts'. I was so embarrassed that for years I would walk with my shoulders curved to hide my chest. Again, did the man who made that disparaging remark think about that moment again? Of course not, but I did.

When caught unaware, these two remarks can still impact the way I relate to my appearance today. I brought them with me and they still impact me today.

This is a good time to remind ourselves that the brain has a negativity bias and remembers the negatives more vividly than positives. I have spent much more time complaining about how unpleasant and annoying people have been towards me than recognising gestures of kindness. I am not reprimanding myself, I just recognise this aspect of being human and maintain awareness of it.

As we grow up, we make many decisions in life based on our expectations of others and ourselves. We build our relationships on the expectations of each other rather than the reality of what we really want or can provide. If those expectations are not met, we are disappointed.

The transition from being a child to being an adult can be rocky. It could be useful to reflect on your defining moments at this stage of your life. Misjudgements made during this time can end up holding us back and hurting us for the rest of our lives.

We all want to love and be loved

I read a book in my early twenties called 'Why Am I Afraid to Love?' which left me with unanswered questions. I now have the main answer, which is because "I did not love myself".

No one can give you self love, without being a good parent to yourself, you will continue to struggle to make meaningful change in your life and overcome the obstacles holding you back. When you love yourself, you can look back at your life without shame, admitting your mistakes and your pain and understanding how they affect your behaviour today.

By loving yourself, caring for yourself and being kind to yourself you also achieve greater independence. You build a solid foundation from which you can explore the world, be loving, caring and kind to people around you without expecting anything in return. This is the unconditional love I want to become a master at.

What about bringing together your defining moments and your irritations to identify the pattern which brought you where you are? It could be very revealing!

Chapter 4
Beliefs and Their Impact on Our Lives

Beliefs shape our lives

Let me now expand on the importance of understanding the impact beliefs have on the quality of your everyday life. They are pivotal influencers to your success or lack of it.

The definition of belief includes being something believed or accepted as true; a mental act, condition or habit of placing trust and confidence in another and as being mental acceptance of a conviction in the truth, actuality or validity of something.

During the first few years of our lives, we believe that anything is possible. We then slowly begin to adopt and acquire other beliefs which we pick up from our parents, peers, teachers and what we see and hear. We believed things when we were children that as adults we know to be untrue. On the other hand, as adults, there are things that we believe now that we never even thought about before.

Children have little or no information with which to analyse situations, and tend to accept external information non-judgementally and are influenced accordingly. As we grow up, some of life's experiences impact us in a negative way. We develop limiting beliefs which can be defined as disempowering generalisations that we make about ourselves, others and our circumstances. We then act as if they are fixed, real and, over time, they become true for us, limiting what we think is possible, how our interactions will unfold and what we can accomplish.

At the same time, we develop empowering beliefs. Instead of hindering healthy and productive thoughts, feelings and actions, empowering beliefs encourage them. They are vital for our individual self-esteem and form the basis of peaceful, cooperative and thriving communities.

Either way, our subconscious mind, which acts as a filing cabinet, is totally non-judgemental and accepts without question the beliefs and stores them in the background of our mind. We get so busy with everything else that we are no longer conscious of these beliefs. However, they are still there and their impact surfaces when we least expect it.

There are therefore two important factors to remember here; the first is that we are not conscious of all the beliefs we have accumulated over the years and, second, that the brain's negativity bias makes it quite challenging to maintain positivity in our everyday lives.

One of the most challenging phenomenon we all deal with, is the tendency to compare ourselves with what other people do or have. This is driven by what we believe about ourselves and about others. This continuous comparison can be very tiring because so often it is driven by those beliefs we have developed over time and that we are not conscious of. They drive our behaviour without us realising it.

To avoid being overwhelmed by your awareness of others and their perceived successes, you need to centre your perspective on yourself and your journey rather than comparing yourself to others. Where are you in relation to where you were? Where are you in relation to where you want to be? These are the only comparisons that matter, and the only ones that will reveal any truth about your life.

Meeting new people and travelling to new places changes your perspective and your beliefs. When I was in Italy, the small area of land around my family's farm was the whole world to me. Then I travelled to London and I encountered an entirely different environment with an entirely different pace of life, full of people from around the globe, each with their own experiences and beliefs of their own. It was, and still is, a continuous, wonderful and enriching experience.

Being exposed to so many different beliefs challenged and broadened my own, as well as making me appreciate aspects of humanity that are shared amongst all of us. Are you aware of your own beliefs?

Thoughts and emotions are symptoms of beliefs

All beliefs, whether limiting or not, form the basis for our thoughts and emotions. Imagine two people are given an identical gift. One of them believes that the gift is valuable, the other believes that it is worthless. Despite the reality that the gift is the same for both of them, the two people will have very different emotional responses to the same gift.

Life gives many of us the same gifts: free will, a world full of opportunities, the ability to connect to other people. Different people will treat these gifts very differently based on their beliefs. Some might think they are doomed to a certain fate, that the world has nothing for them and that other people are untrustworthy whereas others will make use of all the opportunities available. Our entire emotional reality and character grow around such beliefs.

Because thoughts and emotions originate from beliefs, it is more effective to tackle the beliefs causing negative thoughts and emotions than to try to tackle the thoughts and emotions themselves. Think of the thoughts and emotions as symptoms, while the belief is the disease. You can treat the symptoms, but if you do not cure the disease, they will keep coming back.

Be alert - an empowering belief can turn into a limiting belief

Now that I have shared the simple basics of limiting and empowering beliefs, here is the difficult part: it is possible for an empowering belief to become a limiting belief if the circumstances that made the belief empowering in the first place, change.

Here is as an example from my childhood. As the youngest child in a humble family, I was convinced that I was a burden. My family would be horrified if they knew I felt this way, but nonetheless, I was driven to become self sufficient and independent. The belief that I needed to be independent and able to stand on my own two feet was initially empowering. This belief was useful because it pushed me to be courageous and leave home to find new opportunities in London.

However, once I was established and successful, this empowering belief that I used to be independent became a limiting belief. I became unwilling to ask for help and shunned people who might have contributed to my well-being. Looking back, much of that support would have been very welcomed and could have accelerated my development, but at the time I was convinced I needed to go it alone. This caused loneliness, sadness and isolation from the people I would have liked to be close to.

To accept help and support threatened my very identity, the person I considered myself to be. If I was not independent, was I myself anymore? Looking back, I realise that I could have avoided a lot of suffering and unnecessary use of valuable time and energy. Now I can join the dots and take responsibility for the way I acted and use this experience to educate others.

Beliefs that made you successful at one stage in your life may be counterproductive in the next — to continue to be successful, you must make sure that your beliefs are constantly being challenged and refreshed so that you keep moving forward as you develop.

A tough, hardlined attitude might help you get ahead in the corporate world, but what about when you retire and you want to strengthen your bonds with your friends and family? Look ahead to the life you want to live, and ask yourself, will my beliefs help me to get there?

My belief about vulnerability, for example, has changed. Until recently I saw vulnerability as meaning weakness and powerlessness and I would do anything to hide my vulnerability, which manifested as arrogance and dismissiveness.

This has manifested itself when dealing with big projects at work or in the community. If I struggle in keeping things together, the fear of showing my vulnerability brings me to behave in a way which is not conducive to cooperation with others and I could become arrogant and dismissive as a defence mechanism.

I have however, come to realise that vulnerability brings people closer together and enables them to reach a new level of connectedness.

It was a belief formed in my earliest childhood, from my unfounded insecurity about being a burden to my family, that prevented me from realising this earlier, or at least this is what I choose to believe.

I have also come up with what has become one of my own favourite mantras: 'To have a great life is my birthright, vulnerability is part of my greatness and suffering is optional.'

I now invite you to spend a few minutes in looking into your life and identify your major beliefs; look back at your defining moments and join the dots. You will see a pattern emerging which includes both empowering and disempowering beliefs. You can then ask yourself, 'What are my limiting beliefs? what action can I take to start dismantling them?' At the same time though, acknowledge your empowering beliefs and, if necessary, re-commit to them to maintain and enhance the positive impact they have on you.

Chapter 5
Willingness and Responsibility

The buck stops with you

Once you have a clear perspective on where you are and how you got there, along with accepting and learning from your past, the next step is determining how you are going to live in the future. This, above all and in my view, requires willingness and responsibility.

Responsibility has many different meanings. In this context, responsibility means being the cause of change in your life. You are not waiting for circumstances to change around you, you are not waiting for other people to change. Rather, you are developing a clear sense of yourself, your past and your goals so that you can move in the direction you want.

You are also accepting responsibility for the state your life is currently in and the daily decisions you made to get there, good, bad or anywhere in between. Life is like a university, you are here to learn. Look back at your life. Was there a time you stopped doing what mattered to you? If yes, ask yourself why?

We are all torn this way and that by situations and by people, but ultimately we are responsible for our fate. If you are currently unhappy, do not blame yourself, but do not pass on the responsibility either; instead, take hold of it and use it to pull yourself forward.

Owning this responsibility is difficult; at first it can feel like a burden, however, taking sole responsibility for your destiny is empowering, albeit daunting. You take all the victories, but you will also take all the losses. But remember that while you must take sole responsibility for your actions, there are others willing to support you and pick you up when you stumble. To take responsibility is not to go it alone — as I have learned the hard way — it just means that you take control of the decisions that can change your life with the help of people and available resources around you.

Often, the hardest part of starting something is taking the first step. I always remember hearing a marathon runner saying: 'The most difficult part of the training is to put my shoes on.' What is at first difficult will eventually become empowering, and everything after will feel easier in comparison.

Responsibility is the result of being willing

What does responsibility mean in the sense of taking charge of your life and achieving your goals?

Responsibility, ultimately, is the willingness to accept and create change or re-commit to what you already have. It could become a way of life.

Responsibility could be the results of being willing to…

- see your life with a beginner's mind, reassessing your life and your actions with a fresh perspective;

- shed preconceived notions of how the world works, who you are and what you are capable of;

- remove obstacles that prevent you from speaking or acting honestly and freely;

- take a decision when you encounter a difficult choice, rather than avoiding it and returning to what is familiar;

- realise that you are there when problems arise, and therefore share an equal role in the creation and solution of that problem;

- accept help from people who want to see you succeed and wish the best for you, including me!

Willingness is the key. More important than knowing how to do something is the willingness to find out; more important than waiting for evidence, is the willingness to trust others and yourself; more important than being right is the willingness to accept when you may be wrong or misinformed and allow others to contribute to you and correct you.

Living a powerful life is not easy. It may involve facing up to unpleasant situations and finding the courage to communicate with people you perceive as having caused you pain.

You need to understand this and have the willingness to continue, regardless of the difficulties you face and the mistakes you make. If you are unwilling to accept that responsibility, it is unlikely that you will enjoy long lasting change.

Each choice has consequences and each action will bring consequences. Remember, to take no action is still a choice with just as many consequences as taking action — the difference is that you have no real say over those consequences. Is that really what you want?

Resistance is the antithesis of responsibility

You are either willing or resisting; you cannot do both at the same time. The more aware you are of your resistance to something, the more aware you are of your willingness, and vice versa.

All resistance is the result of fear. Whether it is fear of pain, rejection or failure, your brain resists actions that may lead you towards what it subconsciously perceives as a threat. The most basic job of the primary part of the brain is to protect you, to continue your survival. If your life is not in immediate peril, you will be inclined to resist change. After all, if you are already surviving, why risk that by changing?

But this basic instinct does not take your happiness, your mental well-being and your life goals into account. Therefore you need to break this deep instinct of resistance and be willing to change, even if every part of you is screaming for you not to do so.

People who really succeed in life are the ones who break free from their instinct to resist and, instead, take on their responsibilities and make powerful choices towards achieving their goals.

When we take action that comes back to bite us, our tendency is not wanting to take responsibility. Instead, we will blame anyone or anything else rather than admit that we got it wrong. This shifting of blame is a type of resistance, but instead of resisting change, it is resisting the shame and pain of knowing that we did something that either hurt us or others or was not productive.

There is also the other side of the same coin, when we take the blame for everything by invalidating our circumstances or ourselves. This is another aspect of not taking responsibility, on this occasion towards ourselves. It is another version of resistance: the resistance to stand up for oneself because doing so would require confrontation – something I have been guilty of many times.

This is an extension and part of the interaction between the conscious and subconscious part of the mind. There is something in our human machinery that prevents us from dealing with responsibility in a powerful manner.

Admit your mistakes and forgive yourself

Breaking this resistance goes back to self love, and comparing how you would treat others in comparison to how you would treat yourself. Imagine a loved one came to you and admitted they had made a mistake, but they acknowledge that mistake and want to make an honest effort to rectify it. Would you forgive them?

The chances are that you would forgive them, even help them, but would you adopt the same approach towards yourself? We often think mistakes reduce our worth, or make us bad people, so we may avoid admitting to mistakes, both to others and to ourselves. But what if we admitted our mistakes and forgave ourselves like we would a loved one? We could then truly confront what happened, and learn how to avoid making the same mistake again.

The moment I took responsibility for my dissatisfaction and found a new life

I was a troubled teenager. My nickname was 'stubborn' and I was known for being rebellious and difficult. I felt confused, lonely and sad. Looking back, I now know that I caused it. Despite the humble origin, I was surrounded by loving and committed people who always had my best interest at heart, yet I would reject them and on occasions my behaviour was cruel and unhelpful.

The only thing I knew was that I could not make sense of why I felt so lonely while being surrounded by so much love; there was no logic between my emotional experience and the reality around me and the only way I could deal with it was to leave. I craved for freedom, peace of mind and personal power. I took an enormous risk to pack my bags and start searching for them. This search will go on for ever.

I have now accepted that I will always feel dissatisfied to some extent. It does not mean I have not achieved what I want or that I am not happy with my life, it is just a subconscious feeling that is innate in my character. Instead of allowing this feeling to disempower and bring me down like it has in the past, I use it as a source of wonder and excitement to discover what else is available and keep moving forward.

I have also put trust in the universe that I will always find inspiration, as long as I remain open for it. Through understanding this, I am learning to let go of any resistance of how things should or should not be — I say 'learning' rather than 'learned' because this is a lifelong process. I make mistakes like everyone else, but I forgive myself for them and see them as valuable lessons.

Looking back to my teenage years and joining the dots of my life, what stands out is the combination of the unwavering stability my parents and family provided, the values I learned within the community I lived in, my desire to maintain a sense of hope and, finally the curiosity to find out who I could be in the world.

I used to have a poster hanging on my bedroom wall of a girl sitting on the kerb of the road, with her cat on her shoulder. Above her were the words, 'I don't know where I'm going, but I am on my way'.

Fifty years on, that is still true.

Extending the level of responsibility at a community and social level

At a personal level, since I have stopped resisting and started relating to responsibility in an empowering rather than disempowering way, I have committed to becoming a leader in various areas of my life by sharing my own experiences with the view to guide others to take control of their own lives and not fall victim to their circumstances.

This may be easier said than done given what is happening in the world. However, actions taken at a local level will inevitably have a ripple effect in the wider community and the world.

Over the years, I have had the privilege of working with professionals as well as parents, teenagers and young people and have been inspired by the courage and depth of their commitment to create a world that works. I am comforted by the fact that I am in very good company.

I see it as my responsibility to do all I can to empower people within my communities to take on responsibility in a way that would provide what they need to have the life they love.

What commitments are you taking on for your communities? What are you willing to take on that would make a difference?

Chapter 6

Awareness

The truth will set you free

Everything we have covered so far comes under the umbrella of awareness. I want to define awareness as paying attention to your behaviour, being conscious and vigilant of what motivates you and to accept the results of your actions. Awareness is used to shine a light on what is going on in your life.

Awareness of preconceptions

I will start with an example from my own life. It was at a low point in my relationship with my husband, and I was becoming increasingly dissatisfied with our marriage. I could see our relationship going onto a slippery slope. Over a period of time, I put into practice what I have learned and kept stopping by design to ask myself, 'What am I doing? Why am I putting my relationship with my husband and two sons at risk?'

By being painfully honest with myself, I became aware that, regardless of the circumstances, I had a lot to do with the challenges we were facing, without really realising it. I took responsibility for my role in the relationship; I became willing to consider that it was what I had and had not done which had produced these results. I stopped blaming my husband and myself.

My preconceptions of marriage were part of the problem. I discovered that I had an ideal image for what a husband should be, and I was determined to get him to fit into this template. When he did not, I would complain to myself that he was not the way he should be. I was not aware of any of this consciously until I took responsibility and started looking at what was behind my thoughts and actions.

I decided that, instead of trying to fit him into this ideal image I had of how a husband should be, I would try to discover who he was, and appreciate him for the qualities he did have rather than those he did not. We renewed our vows, having first got rid of some of the misunderstandings, misjudgements and preconceptions. We gave ourselves a break!

That was the day I recommitted to our marriage. Over time, our relationship transformed, and through that process of rediscovering my husband, I found all the qualities that I have come to appreciate, love and respect the most. Even though some of his behaviours still irritate me, I now know how to manage them.

I often ask my clients to complete a list of how they would define the ideal partner, father, mother, child, friend, and then ask them to compare that ideal to the type of relationships they have. We develop these ideals and standards unconsciously as we grow up, and while they are necessary to separate the people we like from those we do not, they can also cause distortions that prevent us from communicating effectively with others.

My concept of an ideal husband was not helping me to have a good marriage, instead it was damaging our ability to communicate openly and honestly with each other. By not being aware of our ideals and standards, we run the risk of losing people who could go on to support us achieve our goals and find our purpose.

This is a difficult subject and it has taken me a lot of effort, commitment and soul searching to reach the stage I have. Nevertheless, it is clear evidence that it can be done.

Awareness of mistakes

The pressure not to rattle the cage is so strong that we put up with things that clearly do not work for us and are counterproductive to our development. Sometimes, it is our own cage that we do not want to rattle by admitting that what we do or say is neither helpful nor productive. At some stage we all have not acted authentically towards others to avoid the embarrassment of exposing our weaknesses or misjudgements.

Think of a time when you acted in a way that you felt was inappropriate to someone else. Try to put yourself back in that moment honestly, without reacting with blame or resentment towards yourself or anyone else involved. What emotions preceded your actions? Were those emotions purely related to the situation you were in, or were they rooted elsewhere?

We can acknowledge that we all get worked up about things even if we do not want to and that we follow directions that are not ideal. Nevertheless, we can learn and must learn how to catch ourselves and deal with it.

I call this my umbrella approach. In the same way we use an umbrella to keep dry when it rains, we can develop a strategy to deal with stormy times. So, when you realise that life is stormy, you can rely on your strategy to avoid getting into unworkable situations.

Awareness of the (sometimes difficult) truth

Awareness is part of the process of asking tough questions. Here is one of the well known ones: 'If today was the last day of your life, would you want to be doing what you are doing now?'

If the answer is no, what is driving you to do something that you don't want to do? Are those motivations related to a long term goal (you are not enjoying yourself now, but you will in the future) or is it simply the result of bad habits that you have not had the courage to change?

Be aware that when you ask yourself hard questions, your mind can be evasive and unhelpful, unconsciously steering you to what is easy, not what is consistent with where you want to go. When interrogated, your mind responds with different voices and you need to learn which is your friend and which is your enemy; which one will lead you on your true course and which will lead you astray.

Taking charge of your life means being honest about who you are and what you want. You may think you are being honest to yourself, but if you avoid the difficult questions, perhaps you are not. By being honest about what is important to you, you will naturally work towards creating a positive environment for yourself and people around you.

If these questions are making you feel uncomfortable, then you are feeling the power of resistance at work. Though difficult at first, becoming truly honest about yourself and your desires will make you a happier, more open, more cooperative person. The more you open up to the people around you, the more support and love you will find in the world.

When this cycle of openness and honesty with yourself extends to others, you gain relationships with people who will be willing to be truthful with you because you have displayed that you are truthful with them. This will help on the path of discovery, as no one has a perfect perspective of themselves. By building such relationships with your partner, friends or family, they might tell you about aspects of your character, behaviour or choices that you could never see by yourself.

An example for me was the day I became aware of being a whinger. It was the day when it was pointed out to me that, coupled with the negative bias of our brain, human beings have the automatic tendency to complain. I would start saying, or thinking, this is not fair..... do you remember what you did?........

I started to notice the contents of my conversations when things did not go my way. I realised that, in one way or another, I would complain about most of what was going on in my life.

By becoming aware of what is really going on and using what I have covered so far, I have now accepted that, unless I am aware of what is going on in my head, I have a tendency to complain. And, of course, I now know better!

Awareness of yourself in relation to others

Whether we like it or not, we share the world with other people. We are social creatures: we can only know ourselves in relation to others, whether it is from our interactions or the parts of ourselves we see in other people. Often what we do not like in other people are the things we do not like about ourselves, in this way, other people become our mirror.

You must also be aware of the limits of what other people know about you and your feelings. If you are upset that people are not responding to you the way you want them to, ask yourself the question whether you have made your feelings known. People only know what you share with them, if you block yourself off you cannot be surprised if you often find yourself dissatisfied with their actions.

We all need help; the people who get it are the ones brave enough to ask. If the idea of reaching out to others is making you feel uncomfortable, then, again, you are feeling the power of resistance at work.

How often is your communication based on what you expect to be communicated rather than what is actually being said? I have found myself becoming angry or upset with my husband and then him saying, 'I am not psychic, I did not realise this is what you wanted.' And then it occurs to me that I never said to him what I wanted!

Awareness of mental hygiene

I spend a lot of time making sure I look my best. Washing, grooming, changing clothes are all part of the daily routine which I expect of myself, and others except of me. Physical cleanliness and appearance dictate how we are seen and judged in society and how we draw conclusions about others and their relationship to the world.

I am sure you have your own routine, and would not dare show yourself without first making sure you look how you want to look. My question is, however, how much attention do you give to your mental cleanliness?

The same way as we wash to avoid unpleasant odours, mental clutter gradually builds up until it becomes very uncomfortable. Therefore, like maintaining physical hygiene through daily washing, maintaining mental hygiene is a process of getting rid of unwanted mental clutter.

If I look around my home, I have baskets or rubbish bins in almost every room which are emptied at least once a week. Now, if I picture each part of my life as a room, each one also has its own bin full of clutter, and if I forget to empty the bins, the rooms become more and more unpleasant to be in.

Give yourself some time every day purely focused on putting yourself in the right frame of mind to sort out your thoughts and toss out the unwanted stuff. This process is different for everyone: writing in a journal, meditating, exercising, completing the day, nightly debriefs — whatever helps you reach a mental state that enables you to clearly differentiate the positive, productive parts of your mind from the negative, destructive parts.

I like the famous quote from Buddha: 'Holding onto anger is like drinking poison and expecting the other person to die'. It is our responsibility to deal with our own anger and unhelpful feelings. By holding on to the resentment or by not learning how to forgive ourselves or others, for example, we add to the unnecessary clutter.

Awareness that… emotions are like a plate of spaghetti!

One of my favourite analogies is that emotions are like a plate of spaghetti. Each strand of cooked spaghetti is an individual item, but piled on a plate together they become indistinguishable from one another. The same thing can happen with our emotions. In order to identify what is going on, we must slow down and pick apart the emotions, one at a time and look at where it starts and where it ends.

Nowhere is this truer than within families, where everyone's emotions pile on top of each other for years, even generations. Expectations for how each member of the family should behave were developed as we were growing up, but now they are lost in the mess from years of emotional clutter. But they are still there, in our subconscious, and can show up again when we least expect them. Think of an argument with one of your siblings, for example. You start arguing about something that has just happened and, before you know it, you start bringing up issues that go back years!

Perhaps some of what I have written has irritated you or you do not agree with it. Good. Stop and consider what is behind your reactions and become aware of your own automatic mechanisms. It may well show up things you are not aware of.

Chapter 7
Discover Your Life Purpose

Find the reason you are here

We have now reached the final phase of where I want to take you: how to discover your life purpose. I will define your life purpose as the fulfilment of what you value and treasure in yourself and others. It is based on your beliefs, your values and your commitments. It is the end state you wish to find yourself in, the summary of all the work you have done for yourself and others; it is what you wish to be remembered for.

Discovering your true purpose requires you to take the time to listen to what is really going on within you and what is important to you. There is so much noise and there are so many distractions in daily life that you cannot hear yourself think. It is something you have to make time for, it is not something that you can just slip into a lunch break or hope that it will come automatically.

Although it is challenging to create and maintain a clear sense of purpose, it is your job to, at least, be moving in the direction to where you feel it lies.

Over the years there have been times when I have felt lost and confused, wondering what it is that I live for. Without fail, by reminding myself of what I value the most and what is important to me and then taking consistent action, I find myself back on track.

What has always worked for me has been taking the time to reflect on my progress – or lack of – and see it as a useful feedback system which enables me to plan the next action. My life is not by any means perfect, I have my share of concerns and challenges. What I do find useful though, is the ability to apply what I have shared and regain a sense of equilibrium and peace of mind.

Let me use another analogy I hope you can relate to. Imagine we are all on sail boats. Some people have detailed maps, star charts and compasses that can help them reach their destination, while others have no equipment at all. But no matter how much preparation you make, no one will get anywhere without the wind in their sails. Therefore, the most important thing is to pay attention to the way the wind is blowing, open up your sails and start moving.

Eventually, you will reach somewhere that you feel is perfect for you. For some, it is where they always planned on being, for others it is somewhere they discovered by chance or as a result of a series of coincidences.

At this point it is also important to note that you can spend all the time you like analysing where you are, how you got there and what is going on in your mind, but unless you use your newfound knowledge, skills and perspective to move forward towards your true purpose you are simply squandering your time.

If you are initially not clear of where to start, you can find the tools. With all that is available today in books, on the internet and through educational establishments, there is no excuse for not discovering what can help you. If you are really committed to yourself, it is not a matter of 'if' rather of 'who, where and when'.

Although my purpose has evolved along with my circumstances and lifestyle, it has always been underpinned by curiosity and the desire to feel fulfilled; you have your own version. I started by finding a way to get away from where I was and coming to London, then it was succeeding in my career and raising a happy family, and now it is bringing together all I have learned and sharing it with others so that they too can fulfil what is important to them.

Part of the development and reaching a level of maturity is to learn how to dance with life. There are times when it is necessary to change direction. However, make sure that the change in direction is not an excuse for giving up on the one you were pursuing because the path has become challenging, but rather because the current path is no longer serving you.

I faced such a challenge, another of my defining moments, when I made the transition from being an employee within a large organisation to joining forces with a partner, who happens to be my husband, and becoming self employed.

I found it extremely challenging to make the choice but, remaining where I was, no longer served me. I was afraid of losing out. However, I found the courage to change direction and despite the challenges that followed, I have no regrets.

I am not sure who said, 'Courage is not the absence of fear; courage is the ability to act despite the fear.' These are very wise words. So, rather than trying to leave the fear behind, we can take it with us!

Find and develop the tools

There is no excuse – especially in developed countries – for not finding a way to grow as a person in a way that will positively impact your life, your environment and the communities you are involved with.

I believe there is no right way to find and keep your life purpose alive. There is only your chosen way. There are many tools available to help you stay on course and help you move in your desired direction. Make it your responsibility to find the ones that work for you.

Examples of such tools include:

- *Inspiration*: Few, if any, people are motivated by raw logic alone. No matter how many detailed plans you write, everyone needs inspiration to give them that emotional or spiritual uplift, the excitement of belonging and striving for something different and better. Find stories, people, art or anything else that deeply moves you, and use that feeling to give you the energy to push towards your goals. It is important to be surrounded by people who are inspired by a common goal and help to push you forward.

- *Intentionality*: Be free, be adventurous, but always be deliberate. As much as possible, you must act with intention if you wish to achieve your purpose. Do not allow circumstances to dominate you and do not accept what has become unworkable. By articulating your goals and using them to shape your decisions, you can live proactively by making decisions that change your future, rather than reactively responding to the decisions made by others.

- *Focus*: Everyday life can distract us from our goals, so we need to find ways to constantly remind ourselves of the path we have chosen and avoid being led astray. One very valuable and effective way to keep focused, is having someone to hold you to account. Whether it is someone close to you who has your best interests at heart and wants to see you succeed, or a life coach like me, it makes a real difference to have someone else to remind you of your promises and who believes you can achieve your goals.

- *Measurement:* What do measures consist of? In general, there are two distinct ways to measure what we do. One consists of statistics and tangible results and the other consists of behavioural and intangible results.

  Statistics and tangible results are easily measured. It is the behavioural and intangible measurements that are more difficult to define. Their measurements are subjective and are influenced by the views people hold of themselves and the world. Good examples of these areas are success, acknowledgement and gratitude. The chances are that each person would give different measures.

Sometimes I speak to clients who feel dissatisfied, claiming they have achieved nothing in their life. Then I sit down with them and talk through their lives, and they realise they have achieved so much!

More often than not what has been amiss was not so much the lack of results, rather the way they were measuring their success. They would measure it through the expectations they had of themselves or others or by comparison with others rather than measuring what they have accomplished and where they are now in comparison to where they were when they started.

Without recording when we succeed, reviewing our goals and acknowledging how we contribute to the world on a regular basis, we do not have a clear and objective grasp on how far we have come.

- *Communication:* The development of communication skills is key to personal growth and the fulfilment of your life purpose. Taking action on the back of listening to constructive feedback or coaching on how one communicates can be very useful and speeds up the process of fulfilling your milestones, goals and ultimately life purpose.

One of my defining moments was a time when I was given very useful (and uncomfortable) feedback. It happened during a personal development seminar. It was also the time I understood the meaning of a phrase used fairly often in the world of personal development: 'Yesterday's breakthrough/ success, is tomorrow's ego trip'.

I was surrounded by amazing, successful and inspiring people when I suffered from what I defined an 'ego attack'. I found myself compelled to ensure that the other participants knew how much I had achieved, how successful I had been.

The seminar leader looked at me straight and said: 'So what? Whatever you have achieved is great. However, I would ask you to consider that how you are communicating what you have accomplished is simply a list of what you have done rather than a place of inspiration and fulfilment.'

In that moment, I was able to recognise that because of the environment I found myself in, I had fallen into the trap of comparisons and was communicating coming from a place of insecurity rather than acknowledging my accomplishments so that I could be proud of myself. I admitted the fact that I wanted to cover up one of my limiting beliefs that 'I am not as good as I think I am' and that 'I should do more'. I was comparing my performance to others rather than appreciating my own personal journey and development.

- *Modalities/Techniques:* Nowadays we have the luxury of being able to choose from many modalities to help us to quieten the mind and gain clarity. Some people like running or practicing yoga, while others pursue meditation and mindfulness or participate in seminars and personal training programmes. Additionally, there are a myriad of formally developed healing and well-being techniques for which training is also readily available.

I have trained myself in several techniques which I use for myself and clients. I also pursue physical exercise. I have made some of my best decisions while running.

Each and every one of you can find the necessary tools and create that special space to reflect to enable you to access personal power.

Keep moving

Once you have opened the sails, followed the wind and found the appropriate tools to help you on your journey, you measure your progress.

Finding your life purpose consists of developing a process of self discovery, of personal awareness, of responsibility and of authenticity – being truthful to yourself and others.

I urge my clients to start from wherever they are and move forward and achieve their own short, medium and long term goals; it is in this process that the life purpose will reveal itself. The journey itself will develop who you are, and give quality and flavour to your life.

Often, the final destination will not look like the place you originally expected. This is fairly normal, since the discoveries made during the journey alter the final result. This is a good reason not to become too attached to how things should look, but rather allow new things to evolve naturally.

You may not achieve all your specific goals, but that does not mean you have failed in your purpose.

This takes me back to the way we measure intangible results. As long as you are active in the process of moving towards your goals and consequently your life purpose, you will have succeeded in your development as a person. Growth is not necessarily linear and can be achieved through breakthroughs. Breakthroughs enable the discovery of new paradigms, new worlds and thinking processes which up to that point were unknown to you. Think of the discovery that the earth was round rather than flat, the thinking processes changed in that moment.

So, do not be stuck with the way things should look and be like.

What do I want to leave you with?

My search for my life purpose has been fuelled by a burning desire to experience freedom at a physical, mental and emotional level.

The earliest time I can remember discovering a sense of purpose came after an argument with my mother and sister. I came out of it very upset, and my way of dealing with feeling hurt back then was to withdraw into isolation and wallow in my sad thoughts. I wandered far from the house to find a quiet wall to sit on where I would be all alone. Our village was up in the mountains in the heart of the Apennines and from my wall I had a view over the whole valley. I could see other villages in the distance, little clusters of houses hugging the sides of the mountains that looked tiny from where I was sitting.

I found comfort in the quietness, away from anyone else, watching nature continue its course without any care for me and my troubles. I watched a flock of birds fly over my head all the way to the distant villages, making a journey that would take me all day, look completely effortless. 'What would it be like to be as free as a bird?' I wondered to myself in the silence of the evening.

I realised then that I would never be as free as the birds if I kept withdrawing and isolating myself. I found power in that moment to let go of my sadness and took on the resolve to deal with my circumstances head on so that I could spread my wings and fly beyond them, instead of retreating and becoming stuck in that place.

My circumstances have changed but my approach has remained the same: following a time of crises, I would find a moment of peace and quiet when I would aim to discover what I truly desire, renew my resolve and then act accordingly.

Parallel to my own freedom, over the years I have nurtured and developed the desire to make life work for others too. I find it pointless to be in a position to enjoy life when people around me are miserable or suffering. We are all interconnected. By loving and respecting myself I can love and respect others. I am now in a position where I can teach and support others in loving and respecting themselves.

What also drives me is the belief that we can have a world that works for everyone, where we work together to come up with win-win solutions. It is my life mission to create an environment where we all get to enjoy an ongoing celebration of being involved in the game of life.

Recently, I was asked to define who I considered myself to be, to which I said, 'I am the oil that makes the engine of life work for everyone.'

I love to look at what is happening around me and challenge what is going on, especially when I can detect resignation and when the response is 'This is the way things are, I cannot do anything about it'.

This passion has developed over the years, but where did it begin? I searched my past to find the earliest example where I discovered this desire and it took me all the way back to my first job, working for a marketing company, in a department responsible for processing data used to produce reports at national level.

When I got there, there was already a team who had been working together for some time. They had developed their own processes and rules for how they worked, which they repeated day in, day out without question. This was all new to me, and because of my natural curiosity and cheekiness, I had no reservations about questioning how things were being done.

The response was, 'If you think you could do better, then go ahead!' So I did. They were probably bluffing, but I followed my instincts and logic, using my fresh perspective to identify bottlenecks and bloat in their system. Before long, I had dramatically improved the efficiency of the department, which resulted in the company having their contract renewed.

It was the defining moment when I realised the power of an outsider's perspective and how questioning the way things are done can result in revolutionary discoveries. Office work may be a fairly simple scenario, nevertheless, let's consider that we never know what experiences will change our life, which is why it is important to keep an open mind and do our best at all times.

In that role, I developed an instinct that has remained with me to this day. I cannot look at something without asking what else is possible. I want to make a difference for the better, whether it is a professional organisation or a personal relationship. It is what I do today as a life coach: I use my perspective to listen, then question what is happening and enable clients to take a snapshot of their lives and then provide an approach that empowers them.

No doubt you have your moments too. I invite you to look for them and get in touch with whatever inspired and enabled you to find the courage to take the action that made a difference to you and the people around you. It does not have to be dramatic or unusual; it can come from your daily activities, interactions with strangers or quiet moments of clarity. It is when the light bulb goes on and you get in touch with who you really are.

This, to me, is what it means to reclaim your power and live the life you love.

My final task for you is to put this book down and go to your favourite place to be by yourself, far from all your problems, obligations and distractions. Make yourself comfortable, and ask yourself: 'How did I get here and what do I want for myself?' Then: search, listen, discover, act and enjoy the accomplishments!

I leave you with another of my favourite quotes, this time from Goethe:

Whatever you can do or dream you can,

begin it.

Boldness has genius, power and magic in it!

About the Author

Anna M Stapleton (nee Felli) is an Italian national who has obtained her certification in Life Coaching with Noble-Manhattan. Her extensive professional experience and involvement within the personal growth, training and development industry have equipped her with the necessary skills to offer her services to English and Italian speaking clients around the world.

Anna specialises in mental and emotional freedom coaching and has developed the Defining Moments Coaching Process. This process enables clients to identify defining moments that are at the source of the experience of disempowerment. The process enables the clients to uncover the limiting beliefs developed from these moments and provides the necessary steps to regain power to live a fulfilling life.

"I passionately believe we can have a world that works for everyone. I am committed to a society where win-win situations are the result of working together and it is my life mission to create environments where winning is an ongoing celebration of being involved in the game of life"

Anna M Stapleton

Manufactured by Amazon.com
Columbia, SC
05 April 2017